IMAGES
*of America*

# PARRIS ISLAND

**INSTRUCTION.** Platoon 236 is pictured receiving instructions on pitching shelter halves at Elliott's Beach in 1954.

IMAGES
*of America*

# PARRIS ISLAND

Eugene Alvarez, Ph.D.

ARCADIA
PUBLISHING

Published by Arcadia Publishing
Charleston SC, Chicago IL, Portsmouth NH, San Francisco CA

Printed in the United States of America

Library of Congress Catalog Card Number: 2002100850

For all general information contact Arcadia Publishing at:
Telephone 843-853-2070
Fax 843-853-0044
E-mail sales@arcadiapublishing.com
For customer service and orders:
Toll-Free 1-888-313-2665

Visit us on the Internet at www.arcadiapublishing.com

**PARRIS ISLAND: WHERE IT ALL BEGINS.** The Boulevard de France is the Main Street of the base. The banner above the boulevard reminds all that the two Marine Corps Recruit Depots at Parris Island and San Diego are where one's Marine Corps career begins.

# CONTENTS

# ACKNOWLEDGMENTS

This book is respectfully dedicated to all Marines, recruits, and civilian employees who have briefly, or for a lifetime, called Parris Island home. Their military service and base contributions have earned a reputation for the recruit depot that is enjoyed worldwide.

The author is indebted to the Marine Corps Historical Center in Washington, D.C. for a grant received to research Parris Island's history and significance as a Marine Corps base. I am also indebted to the Parris Island command. One could not have asked for more courtesy and cooperation than the author received while visiting the Parris Island base.

Countless Marines and civilians have contributed information and pictures for this book. Their names are too numerous to mention individually but I am fervently grateful to all. Additional recognition is due to Stephen R. Wise, Ph.D., curator of the Parris Island Museum and to his staff. CWO-2 Phyllis Alexander (USMC Retired) was always attentive to my logistical and research needs. She aided me in many endeavors at the Parris Island base. Phyllis never disappointed me and hers was the "can do" spirit so prevalent among the Marines. Thank you.

I would also like to take this opportunity to thank Pamela Mutch Stevens for directing me to Arcadia Publishing. It was my good fortune to have Laura E. Daniels as my Arcadia book editor. I thank her for her patience and guidance in this endeavor.

Most of the book information and some pictures are taken from two of the author's previous and now out-of-print Parris Island books. Unless otherwise noted, picture credits are due to the Department of Defense, Parris Island Public Affairs Office, Parris Island Photograph Training Support Center, and the Parris Island Museum. Photographs taken by the author are not credited.

# INTRODUCTION

The United States Marine Corps Recruit Depot, Parris Island, South Carolina is one of the most famous military bases in the world. The post has been the subject of numerous books and motion pictures, television presentations, and poems. Young men and women who have received their recruit training here ("boot camp") have never forgotten the base where youthful innocence was lost. It is also at Parris Island, one of the two Marine Corps Recruit Depots, where one earns the prestigious title of United States Marine.

The Native Americans, French, Spanish, and English have all inhabited Parris Island at one time or another and Parris Island was also a part of the Southern Confederacy during the American Civil War. Col. Alexander Parris (1662–1736) purchased land on the island in 1715 and the island is named after him. Through World War I, the Parris name was incorrectly spelled Paris. The Marine Corps corrected the error in 1919, and the proper spelling of Parris, with two *R*s, has been used since.

The United States Marine Corps Recruit Depot is in Beaufort County, South Carolina. It is approximately four miles long and three miles wide. The base is surrounded by Port Royal Harbor, the Beaufort and Broad Rivers, and includes such primary waterways as Archer's, Ballast, and Ribbon Creeks.

Parris Island consists of about 8,000 acres of land, of which approximately 4,400 acres are dry and suitable for the training mission and the maintenance of the base. Most of Parris Island is only a few feet above sea level. However, an elevation of near 21 feet above sea level exists on Horse Island and in the vicinity of the Third Recruit Training Battalion Physical Training Field.

Parris Island occasionally receives snow and at times ice storms, but it is more renowned for its insects, humidity, and heat. Hurricanes can be a major threat to the South Carolina coast. An 1893 hurricane and tidal wave inundated Parris Island on August 28. Several thousand people perished at this time along the South Carolina coast. A 1940 hurricane wrecked much of the causeway and the base and several other hurricanes have caused extensive damage.

Venomous reptiles on Parris Island include the rarely encountered but very lethal coral snake, the copperhead, the dangerous cottonmouth water moccasin, and the eastern diamondback rattlesnake. These poisonous reptiles have been found mostly on the base golf course, at Elliott's and Niver's Beaches, and at Page Field. On one instance, nine snakes were killed on the golf course in one day. The largest recorded rattlesnake was killed near the base Argonne Trailer Park in 1981. The dispatched "rattler" appeared to be a log in the roadway and its length measured better than seven feet.

Alligators also inhabit the base. They have been known to venture onto the Parris Island golf course and into training areas. A few alligators, usually following hurricanes or rainstorms, have even been seen on the parade field in the past. Other wildlife includes rabbit, deer, otter, squirrels, and raccoons. Birds in the vicinity include the Eastern Brown Pelican, egret, heron, osprey, sandpiper, and numerous species of diving, wading, and "fishing" birds. Parris Island's wild and domestic plants, trees, and shrubs are as varied as the animal life. So many cedar trees once grew on the island that Cedar Island was a former Parris Island name. Cotton was once grown on Parris Island and orange trees were evident as late as World War II. Ragweed, poison ivy, oak, sumac, poinsettias, and milkweed also inhabit the vicinity. Colorful and large oleander bushes once lined the causeway from the base gate to Archer's Creek.

Today, Parris Island is a protected refuge for sea and animal wildlife. The historic island and base is not only vital to the nation's defense, but is also one of the most beautiful posts of the United States Marine Corps.

**MODERN PARRIS ISLAND.** The Marine Corps Recruit Depot constantly changes. Recruits from as recent as the Vietnam War have difficulty locating their old training site. This picture shows the base brick barracks and a parade deck that is used for recruit platoon graduation exercises. (Photo by Ernest Ferguson.)

# One

# THE EARLY YEARS
## 1562–1917

*Soon after Christopher Columbus discovered America, other Spanish explorers sailed along the southeastern United States coast. The Spanish named the present Parris Island vicinity Santa Helena (St. Elena) in 1525. The French challenged Spain's North American presence in 1562. That year Jean Ribaut (Ribault) visited Port Royal Harbor to claim the lands for France. Ribaut described the harbor as one of "beauty and grandeur" where "without danger, all the ships in the world might be harbored." Ribaut named the magnificent harbor Port Royal.*

*The names Port Royal and Parris Island can be confusing. It should be noted that Port Royal was, and is, both the name of the great harbor and the name of the nearby town. The Parris Island base was referred to as Port Royal until 1917. For purposes of this book, the names Parris Island and Port Royal will be used interchangeably.*

**MAIN GATE.** The Parris Island main gate has been relocated and altered many times. Most recently, the entrance has been modernized and made more colorful and secure. (Courtesy of CWO-2 Phyllis Alexander, USMC, Retired.)

Portus Regalis, siue F.S.Helenæ

**FIRST STRUCTURE ON PARRIS ISLAND**

**PORT ROYAL HARBOR, 1562.** This early map of Port Royal Harbor pictures two ships anchored (center left) off Parris Island. A third vessel is entering Port Royal Harbor.

**AN ARTISTIC CREATION OF CHARLESFORT.** The Europeans quickly built a small wilderness outpost that they named Charlesfort. In 1563, the remaining and disenchanted French abandoned Charlesort to return to Europe in a crudely built ship.

**THE RIBAUT MONUMENT.** It is believed that the French erected a marker at Charlesfort to claim the lands for France. A modern column marks the site today.

RIBAUT LANDING
First Ship Built in America
Beaufort - Parris Island, South Carolina

PARRIS ISLAND S.C.
MAY 19
11:30 AM
1938

AIR MAIL

6¢ UNITED STATES 6¢

"Where History Begins"
— 1562 —
Air Mail Week May 15-21, 1938

Miss Katharine Glancy
U. S. Naval Hospital
Quantico.
Virginia.

**FIRST SHIP BUILT IN THE UNITED STATES.** Some of the Frenchmen did not survive their return voyage to Europe. Cannibalism was practiced among the men at sea. It is likely that their Parris Island vessel was the first ocean-going ship built by Europeans in the United States. This claim has often been stated, such as on a Parris Island envelope that was mailed to Quantico, Virginia, in 1938.

11

**SEARCHING FOR REMAINS.** It was long alleged that Charlesfort was built on or near the site of today's Ribaut Monument. It is possible that the fort site could have been washed away over the centuries, or that the fort was built at another place. Most recent archaeological examinations seem to confirm that the French settlement was indeed in the Parris Island golf course area, where Charlesfort's location is confirmed today.

*B. V. A. Arsenal, Beaufort, S. C.*

19

**THE BEAUFORT ARSENAL.** Parris Island's nearby town of Beaufort was settled in 1711. Fort Frederick was built near the town on the banks of the Beaufort River in 1731. The fort was abandoned in 1758. Little action occurred near Beaufort during the American Revolution but one reminder of that time is the Beaufort Volunteer Arsenal. The arsenal was organized two months before the Declaration of Independence signing in 1776 and has also housed the Beaufort Museum and Relic Room.

**PARRIS ISLAND CABIN.** Parris Island supported at least five antebellum plantations owned by notable families in the history of the state. They include the Barnwells, Elliotts, Graysons, Habershams, and Eddings. The families collectively possessed approximately 500 slaves who mostly lived in small, austere, frame homes. Notice the pail hanging on the side of this house.

13

**CEMETERY.** It is probable that some Parris Island slaves or their descendants are buried in a small cemetery that is located near the base rifle range. This 1981 photograph identifies a few of the remaining and standing gravestones. Other Parris Island cemeteries have been lost in time.

**BATTLE OF PORT ROYAL, 1861.** Port Royal's military significance was quickly realized at the onset of the 1861–1865 Civil War. Adm. Samuel F. Du Pont won a major naval engagement against Confederate shore batteries on November 7, 1861, at the Battle of Port Royal. Hilton Head and Beaufort became important Union military bases. A naval coaling station was operational on Parris Island by the end of the Civil War. The fuel facility was the first federal installation on Parris Island, which eventually became home to the United States Marine Corps Recruit Depot.

**LT. CHARLES H. LYMAN, USN.** Port Royal's first commanding officer was Charles H. Lyman. Lieutenant Lyman entered the naval service in 1866 and had an illustrious, yet sometimes stormy, career. He died on January 28, 1897. (Courtesy of Col. Andrew I. Lyman, USMC, Retired.)

**THE LYMAN FAMILY AT PARRIS ISLAND.** This 1924 photograph pictures Lieutenant Lyman's son and the grandchildren. Pictured from left to right are David Hinckley Lyman (colonel), Charles H. Lyman II (later major general), Charles H. Lyman III (later rear admiral, USN), Mrs. Charles H. Lyman, and Andrew I. Lyman (later colonel). Charles H. Lyman II served several tours of duty at Parris Island commanding the Marine barracks and as base chief of staff. As a major general, Charles H. Lyman II was the first commanding general of the Fleet Marine Force (FMF) that was formed in 1933. (Courtesy of Col. Andrew I. Lyman, USMC, Retired.)

**PARRIS ISLAND DRY DOCK.** Construction on a massive naval station dry dock began in 1891, but a hurricane and tidal wave inundated the island in 1893 and damaged the dock. An estimated 2,000 lives were lost between the Savannah River and the North Edisto Inlet. One Parris Island woman recorded, "Nearly half the people on Parris Island perished that awful night." President Grover Cleveland rushed supplies to residents, and Clara Barton, American Red Cross founder, visited the Carolina coast. This photograph is dated August 29, 1895, the year of the dock's completion. Today's commanding officer's home, designated Quarters One, is the two-story house to the left.

**PARRIS ISLAND DRY DOCK, 1895–1896.** This photograph shows a ship in dry dock and prepared for maintenance work. Most of the homes in the background remain today. They are on the National Register for Historic Places, as is most of the dry dock area.

**USS INDIANA.** Some of the largest ships in the United States Navy used the Port Royal Naval Station Dry Dock. The battleship *Indiana* is pictured here.

**FIRST BASE HEADQUARTERS BUILDING.** This frame building is believed to have served as the initial Naval Station Headquarters for Lieutenant Lyman. The building was near the dry dock, but was later moved or incorporated into other buildings. Quarters One, the present commanding general's home, is seen in the right center of the photograph. (Courtesy of Col. Andrew I. Lyman, USMC, Retired.)

**PORT ROYAL NAVAL STATION DRY DOCK.** Vessels entered the facility from the Beaufort River. A huge iron door sealed the slip and powerful cetrifugal pumps emptied it. Water may have been trapped between the smaller and larger parts of the slip. The iron door was removed to allow the exit of a ship. This photograph clearly shows the wooden timbers and the size of the slip. The single house to the left of the picture is the Parris Island commanding general's current residence. Other large homes are hidden behind the railroad crane and they remain today.

**QUARTERS ONE.** This home is the residence of the Parris Island commanding general and family. It is one of the oldest structures on the base and is on the National Register of Historical sites.

**THE SEA ISLAND HOTEL.** The former Beaufort Sea Island Hotel was built in 1820. The building served as the federal Army headquarters during the War Between the States. It was used into the late 1950s as a Bay Street hotel.

**PORT ROYAL, SOUTH CAROLINA—THE NEW UNITED STATES NAVAL STATION.** A Port Royal coaling station was operational in 1876. An island lighthouse was built in 1881 to assist ships in navigating the harbor. In 1882, the government was committed to a Parris Island Naval Station. In 1890, an appropriation for $200,000 was allotted for the construction of a Parris Island timber dry dock. On June 26, 1891, the United States Naval Station, Port Royal, South Carolina was formally dedicated.

**MACHINE SHOP.** A large crane and machine shops served the dry dock. The long center pictured building is now the Depot Lyceum. The former base headquarters building is to the left of the machine shop, or the present Lyceum. Two sections of the dry dock are well defined.

**DECORATED LYCEUM.** In later years, the machine shop was designated the Lyceum. The large building was and is used for many events. This 1924 photograph pictures the spacious interior decorated for a Christmas event. Parris Island's first motion pictures were shown here and a projection booth is visible in the photograph. (Courtesy of Col. Andrew I. Lyman, USMC, Retired.)

**RIDING THE RANGE.** Although there was much activity around the dock, the Naval Station remained a small base. Hunting and horseback riding were popular. Notice that two of the riders are mounted on cows. The Beaufort River is in the background. (Courtesy of Col. Charles I. Lyman, USMC, Retired.)

THE PARRIS ISLAND DRY DOCK TODAY. The facility was deactivated by 1909, and was replaced by a Charleston dock. The Parris Island timbers were concreted over in later years, but barge and other traffic used the former dry dock into the 1960s and 1970s. Today, the slip is filled with mud. Two of the original Naval Station buildings are seen in the immediate background.

SPANISH-AMERICAN WAR. Parris Island's first war was the brief 1898 Spanish-American War. Gun batteries protected the Port Royal Harbor entrance, as other batteries did, along the southeastern United States coast. This emplacement was at the north end of Hilton Head Island, across from Parris Island. The battery became a victim to tides and hurricanes over the years.

**FORT FREMONT.** The massive Fort Fremont was quickly constructed to protect the Beaufort River during the 1898 Spanish-American War. In 1957, the area was neglected and covered in brush.

Pan. of Naval Station, Port Royal, S. C.

**PORT ROYAL NAVAL STATION.** This panoramic picture of the Naval Station was taken from near the present Commanding General's Headquarters. Notice the outhouses behind two of the officers' quarters. The two large brick buildings are Numbers 10 and 11. They are two of the

**PORT ROYAL NAVAL STATION.** In 1900, Parris Island remained an isolated naval station that was only connected to the mainland by telegraph. Notice the white fence on the other side of the large, two-story house that surrounded much of the base. Civilians, including numerous black families, inhabited the remainder of the island until their removal on the eve of World War II.

oldest structures on the Parris Island base and both are still in use today. The Beaufort River is in the distance. (Courtesy of Dwight Stuckey.)

**MARINE OFFICERS SCHOOL, PORT ROYAL, 1909.** With the transfer of dry dock needs to Charleston in 1909, a short-lived school for Marine Corps officers was formed at Parris Island. The purpose of the school was to indoctrinate and train newly commissioned officers. Many future and famous general officers attended the Port Royal school. In 1910 to 1911, brief efforts were attempted to begin recruit training on Parris Island. Only a very small number of men were trained on the base at this time. In 1911, the recruit training was relocated to Charleston, South Carolina, and later to Norfolk, Virginia, where it remained until 1915.

UNITED STATES NAVAL DISCIPLINARY BARRACKS, PORT ROYAL. In 1911, Parris Island received over 300 naval prisoners. Most were not violent men and were confined to Parris Island for no more than three years. Rehabilitation was emphasized rather than punishment. Escape from the island was nearly impossible. This image pictures a review of sailors and Marines on the site of the present Headquarters & Service Battalion along the Boulevard de France. Buildings 10 and 11 are prominent in the photograph and remain in use today. (Courtesy of Dwight Stuckey.)

BOAT DRILL. The boat drill is in the station dry dock and on the reverse side of Buildings 10 and 11. The water tank remains visible. The gazebo that is at the head of the slip now stands on the other side of the flagpole near the general's residence, Quarters One. The disciplinary barracks were closed in 1933. (Courtesy of Dwight Stuckey.)

THE GAZEBO. This 1920s photograph clearly shows the flagpole and reveals that the base gazebo was moved to the corner of the street. Quarters One is across the street. A small corner of the dry dock is seen in the picture at center-left.

OFFICERS QUARTERS, UNITED STATES NAVAL DISCIPLINARY BARRACKS. This charming photograph pictures a cow grazing near the Officers Quarters. The image shows the front of the houses that are pictured from the rear in other photographs. Several of the homes still stand on Tripoli Street. The corner of Building 11 is seen in the background. Low-lying base grounds, such as seen in the foreground, were common to Parris Island and were filled with soil in later years. (Courtesy of Dwight Stuckey.)

**MAIN STATION.** Following the transfer of dry dock duties, the Port Royal main station remained an active base, as revealed in this photograph. The Beaufort River is in the background. Attention was again resurrected to the possibility of Parris Island being used as a primary base to train recruits.

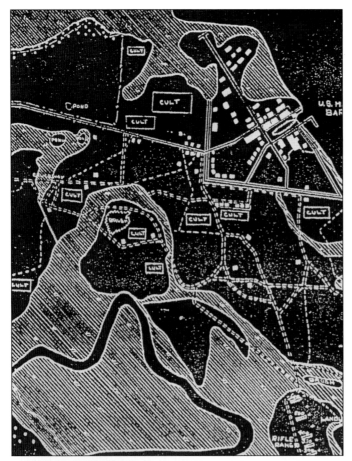

**PARRIS ISLAND, 1916.**
Parris Island became a
Marine Corps base on
October 25, 1915, after the
USS *Prairie* transferred
the men and baggage
from Norfolk, Virginia
to the small and remote
South Carolina base. The
old gunboat transported
prisoners from the
disciplinary barracks to
Norfolk. Several voyages
were made. Parris Island
was now named "Marine
Barracks, Port Royal." This
1916 map shows a fence
enclosing the main station.
The dry dock is clearly
visible. Notice the initial
base rifle range. The large
area in the upper-left
corner is the parade ground
vicinity. It is bordered on
the south side by what
will eventually be the
Boulevard de France.

**BOULEVARD DE FRANCE.** One of the most pressing problems for the new base was to build
Parris Island roads. The eventual main thoroughfare was and is the Boulevard de France. The
1916 Marines did not realize that the boulevard would be as beautiful as it is today, and that the
roadway would honor the Marines of the first World War.

# *Two*

# WORLD WARS I AND II
## 1917–1949

*Most 1917–1918 recruits were trained at Parris Island during World War I. It has been observed that, "one of the outstanding characteristics of the Recruit Depot on Parris Island has been its ability to expand and contract in size, as time and conditions require." However, the large influx of recruits caused many problems for the young and growing base. Two of these were the disposal of raw sewage and the island's need for food and a fresh water supply. The mailing address, Marine Barracks, Port Royal, caused hundreds of letters to be inadvertently received in the nearby town of Port Royal. The confusion was mostly eliminated in June 1917, when the base name was changed to Marine Barracks, Paris Island.*

**MEXICO STREET.** During World War I the street was a busy Parris Island thoroughfare. Note the traffic shelter and the nearby truck. Buildings 10 and 11 are clearly visible. A group of Marines is passing in review. The other formation is at present arms.

**YEMASSEE STATION.** Young men came from many parts of the nation, especially east of the Mississippi River, to join the Marines and to "make the world safe for democracy" in World War I. Transportation was primarily by rail. Yemassee, South Carolina was the nearest mainline station to Beaufort, Port Royal, and Parris Island.

**WORLD WAR I RECRUITS.** Recruits arrived by boat from the mainland to Parris Island before the base was connected to the mainland. From the post dock, the "boots" were confined to a quarantine station for several days before entering the training program.

**MARCHING TO THE MANEUVER GROUNDS.** The lot of the World War I recruit was demanding and rigorous. Salt water was utilized except for drinking and cooking purposes. A fresh water shower was rare. Body lice were common. Unpaved roads were the norm for the base, and the large parade field was not paved until World War II. One general officer later commented that people "could hardly believe" the stories that were heard about recruits, who scooped up buckets of oyster shells with their bare hands to be used for the foundation of base roads.

**PARRIS ISLAND CANTONMENT.** Temporary buildings and tents created a base cantonment that received approximately 46,000 World War I recruits. Many of these men achieved future fame. Edwin Denby became President Warren G. Harding's secretary of the Navy. Gene Tunney trained at Parris Island and defeated Jack Dempsey to become the undefeated heavyweight boxing champion of the world. Bob Burns became a famous entertainer and musician. Burns invented an instrument that he named the Bazooka and that name was used to identify an anti-tank weapon in later wars.

**MARKSMANSHIP.** The Marine Corps has always prided itself on having some of the finest marksmen in the world. A Marine never called his rifle a gun. To do so could cause a severe reaction from a drill instructor (DI). Should a recruit drop his rifle, he could be ordered to sleep with the weapon. One wag wrote, "Your rifle is your best friend; take care of it. Treat it as you would your wife. Rub it thoroughly with an oily rag every day!" This photograph pictures recruits in the prone position at the 500-yard line. Rifle coaches are seated to the rear.

**RIFLE RANGE.** This is a collection of rifle range photographs, including World War I rifle and pistol shooters, barracks, and rifle targets and butts.

**RIFLE RANGE TARGET CARRIAGES.** In between prescribed firing times, targets were lowered by carriages behind the earthen butts. Targets were marked and shots were scored by the shooters. To completely miss the target was to earn a red flag signal called "Maggies Drawers." The picture shows targets in the air and the chain mechanism used to lower them. Target pullers are safe behind the protective butts. Shooters and pullers exchanged positions so that all fired the rifle.

**PISTOL RANGE.** Recruits were instructed on the use of the pistol as well as the rifle. This photograph shows the shooter, a seated coach, and a scorekeeper behind each shooter tending to a scoreboard. Safety on the firing line was essential and important above all else.

**BAYONET COURSE.** Bayonet training provides stamina and confidence. A threat of cold steel also served for psychological purposes on the World War I battlefield.

**FREE TIME.** Recruits of any era have little free time. An exception is this day off for the Fourth of July. Notice the tent living quarters.

**INSPECTION.** Inspections are frequent in recruit training. The rifle inspection requires the inspecting officer to take the weapon and examine the chamber and other parts of the rifle for dirt or rust.

**PASSING IN REVIEW.** Graduation is the day awaited by all recruits. The event was often marked by a parade or a review, even during times of war. Notice the horses, the dog, and the sand parade field.

**POST DOCKS.** A decade would pass after the war before the Parris Island base would be connected to the mainland. The post dock and its tugs were very essential to the post. Notice the smaller barge to the left of the tug *Kite*.

**POST-WAR.** Parris Island quickly returned to normal after the war, but had grown larger than both the towns of Port Royal and Beaufort combined. This photograph pictures several autos and Buildings 11 and 10. The gazebo, as it is today, sits at the head of the dry dock.

**METAL HANGAR.** This metal hangar near the marina may have been brought to Parris Island from Nicaragua during the early 1930s. Other hangars were also here until they were demolished or badly damaged by hurricanes. The pictured building was razed in 2001 along with the other large building.

**AVIATION ONLOOKERS.** The first aviation unit arrived on Parris Island in 1919. Landings were done on any flat land, and even on the base parade field. Seaplanes later landed in the marina area. The first plane to arrive on the base may have been a DH-4 that was piloted by Lt. Ford O. "Tex" Rogers. The pictured plane is unidentified. It appears that an important discussion is in progress near this vintage airplane.

**PILOTS.** These aviators posed for a group photograph on Parris Island. Notice how closely the flight uniforms resemble those of World War I. Landings at Parris Island were associated with several record flights.

**LIGHTER THAN AIRSHIPS.** Dirigibles or "lighter than airships" landed at Parris Island in the late 1920s and perhaps early 1930s. Mooring masts were erected near the marsh at the end of Santo Domingo Street and later at Page Field. The mooring mast is seen at the front (bow) of the dirigible in this photograph. Airships that landed at Parris Island include the *Macon*, the *Akron*, and the *Los Angeles*.

MOORING MAST. This 1939 photograph shows the site of the mooring mast at the end of Santo Domingo Street. The spot is identified by the white circle just left of the center of the photograph. The parade field is in the upper left of the picture and the dry dock area is in the upper right.

AIRSHIP LOS ANGELES. The Los Angeles attracted numerous curious onlookers while moored at Parris Island. The crew and passengers rode in the area married to the bottom of the ship. Following several tragic explosions, the dirigible program was curtailed.

**FIRST AUTOMOBILE.** It is uncertain when the automobile first arrived on Parris Island. There are reports of vehicles on the island before World War I. This picture records one of the earliest cars on the base being driven by aviator Lt. Ford O. "Tex" Rogers.

**PARRIS ISLAND CAUSEWAY.** It was necessary for Parris Island to be connected to the mainland in order to become a major military base. Construction began on a causeway to link the base with Jericho Point and Burton Road in 1923. Heavy earth-moving and dredging equipment was brought to the vicinity and disciplinary barracks prison labor was used. Machines were lost in the salt marsh and prisoners were given credit for two days on their sentence for each one-day worked on the causeway. This photograph shows the new one-lane causeway that reached Archer's Creek in 1927. Because of the present dangers, many continued to use water transportation to and from the base.

**PARRIS ISLAND CAUSEWAY.** This much later photograph pictures the causeway up to Archer's Creek and Horse Island. Notice the simple main gate and the large guardhouse and barracks that were constructed in World War II.

**ARCHER'S CREEK FERRY.** A ferry was used to cross Archer's Creek until the construction of an Archers Creek Bridge. Old-timers on Parris Island recall that the posts appearing in the marsh and on the creek bank were once part of the Parris Island ferry operation. The current causeway can be seen to the left leading to the main gate.

**ARCHER'S CREEK BRIDGE.** The mainland and the base were completely joined by a steel bridge that opened for traffic on December 5, 1928. During World War II, a narrow, wooden bridge was constructed adjacent to the steel bridge. Traffic was one way on each bridge.

**HORSE ISLAND GATE.** After a bridge was constructed to join the island and the causeway, a main gate was opened on Horse Island. Notice the artillery piece in front of the far stop sign. The truck would be approaching Archer's Creek. Horse Island is in the background.

**CAUSEWAY AND ARCHER'S CREEK.** This recent photograph shows the causeway, Archer's Creek, and Horse Island in the tree line. The pictured modern bridge was dedicated on September 30, 1954. To one side of the modern bridge the old bridge roadway is visible. Oleander bushes once lined the causeway.

**IRON MIKE.** Parris Island's *Iron Mike* was unveiled in 1924. The statue was sculpted by World War I veteran Robert Ingersoll Aitken (1878–1949) and was financed through the subscriptions of World War I Marines. New York's Rowan Bronze Works cast the statue. The unveiling occurred in front of the first Parris Island Hostess House, Post Inn.

**DEDICATION OF *IRON MIKE*.** The statue originally stood on present Panama Street, west of the Parris Island Museum. It was initially placed at this location so that all recruits who departed Parris Island "must pass by this inspiring piece of art." The panoramic photograph, of which

the left half appears above, shows the current First Battalion area to the far left. The main road running through the picture is the Boulevard de France. Beyond the right side of the photograph is the site of the present Marine Corps Exchange.

**STATUE RELOCATION.** On the eve of World War II, Panama Street was extended to allow the construction of the Second Recruit Training Battalion. *Iron Mike* was moved to the present site on the Boulevard de France. The initial Hostess House was removed and a new World War II Inn was built near by. The Temporary Lodging Facility is the third such base facility.

**IRON MIKE.** This impressive statue remains as a reminder of the "Devil Dog" Marines who died in World War I. The statue inscription reads, "In Memory Of The Men Of Parris Island Who Gave Their Lives In The World War. Erected By Their Comrades."

**RIBAUT MONUMENT.** A monument was placed near or on the site of Charlesfort in 1926. Approximately 200 visitors attended the ceremonies, including Maj. George H. Osterhout Jr., who was mostly responsible for pursuing the location of the French fort. Others attending were Secretary of the Navy Curtis D. Wilbur and Marine Corps commandant John A. Lejeune.

**RIBAUT MONUMENT.** This impressive shaft reminds us today of the earliest Parris Island history. A nearby display honors the relationship between Spain and the United States.

**BASE HEADQUARTERS.** Until World War II, this building served as the base headquarters. The brick building is adjacent to the Lyceum and dates back to naval station days.

**SUNDAY SCHOOL CLASS.** This is a photo of a Parris Island Sunday School class in 1924. Notice the Marine is wearing leggings and seems to enjoy being among the children. (Courtesy of Col. Andrew I. Lyman, USMC, Retired.)

**PARRIS ISLAND STAFF.** Brig. Gen. Harry Lee and his staff are pictured here in 1925. Lee commanded the depot from 1924 to 1927, and from 1929 to 1933. The picture was taken in front of the former base headquarters building.

**FIELD MUSIC SCHOOL.** The base Field Music School trained buglers who had to master numerous bugle calls. Buglers were used on the base as late as the early 1950s.

PARRIS ISLAND, C. 1925. This photograph shows much of the remaining waterfront World War I cantonment and the East Wing area that was once on the present parade field. The long Boulevard de France (center) ends well before Horse Island since Archer's Creek has yet to be spanned. Panama Street (lower center left) has yet to be extended. The dry dock is seen in the lower right side of the photograph.

PARRIS ISLAND APRIL 22, 1931. By 1931, little construction had been done on the base south of the main station to Ballast Creek. Notice the large stack that was once near the dry dock.

PARADE DECK AREA, APRIL 22, 1931. By 1931, much of the World War I waterfront cantonment had been removed. The East Wing is on the southeast end of the parade field. Little was in the present Second Battalion area.

THE EAST WING. By the 1930s, most recruit training was conducted in the East Wing. The barracks were located near the waterfront in the present First Recruit Training Battalion Physical Training Field.

**EAST WING BARRACKS.** This 1932 East Wing building was common housing for recruit training during the 1930s and to the eve of World War II. Most of the barracks were destroyed by a monstrous hurricane that struck Parris Island in 1940. (Courtesy of Walter Wilson.)

**RECRUIT BARRACKS.** Recruits were also housed in barracks that stood on the present site of the Headquarters and Service Battalion along the Boulevard de France. Notice the concrete wash rack and that recruit clothing is elevated on lines to prevent theft. Only the drill instructor had the key to open a locked box, from which the clothing could be lowered. (Courtesy of Master Sgt. Sam Cosman, United States Army, Retired.)

**PVT. SAM COSMAN.** Recruiting during the Depression years was very select—perhaps moreso than at any other time in the Marine Corps. Pictured is Pvt. Sam Cosman who graduated from recruit training in 1938. Notice the Springfield '03 rifle, leggings, cartridge belt, and pack with the bayonet attached. Cosman saw action throughout the Pacific War and finished his military career in the United States Army. (Courtesy of Master Sgt. Sam Cosman, United States Army, Retired.)

**MAIN STATION AREA, 1939.** This photograph records the construction of the Headquarters and Service Battalion along the Boulevard de France. The present base theater sits on the water tank site. A new commanding general's headquarter building was not yet constructed.

**NEARLY COMPLETED HEADQUARTERS AND SERVICE BATTALION, 1940.** The H&S Battalion is nearly complete, but is missing an attached mess hall to the center rear of the building. Many World War II recruits first arrived at Parris Island at this building, until they were assigned to a recruit training battalion. Notice the absence of the *Iron Mike* statue across from the water tank.

RIFLE RANGE HEADQUARTERS. A new rifle range headquarters building was under construction in 1939 and was completed in 1940. Notice the old barracks. A huge, indoor swimming pool for recruit training was soon built facing the road, to the left in the picture. Wake Boulevard is seen in the picture to the right.

HEADQUARTERS BUILDING. This is a photo of the completed rifle range headquarters building facing Wake Boulevard. Notice the long screened porches for the barracks areas that helped keep the squad bays cool from the heat.

**PARRIS ISLAND TENTS.** By 1940, many realized that the United States would be drawn into a second World War. Recruit arrivals greatly increased and base construction was evident everywhere. Non-base related civilians were removed from the Recruit Depot, and the entire island was acquired by the government of the United States. Many recruits were placed in tents as new barracks were under construction. Tents have frequently been used on the Recruit Depot in times of tremendous recruit loads. Notice the wooden locker boxes, cots, galvanized pail, and ankle-high field boots the Marines wore into the early 1950s and the Korean War. (Courtesy of Maj. Perry Coley, USAF, Retired.)

**Hurricane of 1940.** Parris Island was damaged by another monstrous hurricane on August 11, 1940. The East Wing barracks were wrecked and the base causeway was partly awash. Aircraft hangars were demolished and the wooden flooring of recruit tents floated to other islands nearby.

**Hurricane of 1940.** The Recruit Depot suffered at least $1,500,000 in damages. Unlike the 1893 hurricane, no lives were lost. This photograph shows a stripped Quartermaster building.

EVOLUTION OF A BATTALION. Work rapidly progressed on the First Battalion in 1940. Notice the temporary tents on the sand parade field in the lower right corner. It appears that artillery pieces are on the field near the tents. The Boulevard de France is in the lower left corner of the photograph.

NEAR COMPLETION OF THE FIRST BATTALION. This 1940 photograph pictures the near completion of the First Battalion. More buildings were later added adjacent to the last shown building that is an old barracks of the East Wing. A former fire station is seen on the Boulevard de France where the thoroughfare joined Malecon Drive. In 2001, the boulevard was terminated with curbing at the juncture with Malecon Drive. It is Malecon Drive that leads to the main gate.

FIRST AND SECOND BATTALION AREAS, 1944. Three World War II H-designed barracks and one mess hall appear in the First Battalion area along the waterfront. The western end of the parade field and the Boulevard de France are in the center of the photograph. At the far right, the square building is the recruit Triangle PX that remained in use for years. Notice the large numbers of metal Quonset huts along side the Boulevard de France. The huts were removed after the war. Many of them were most likely placed in the present commissary and Third Battalion area. Second Battalion barracks, a mess hall, and supply buildings are in the upper part of the photograph. The two white objects on the parade field are movable basketball boards. Notice the one marching platoon on the parade field.

**RETIREMENT PARADE.** This 1944 photograph pictures the retirement parade for Brig. Gen. Emile P. Moses, who commanded the Parris Island base from 1941 to 1944. Notice the parade field is now paved. Automobiles are parked along the Boulevard de France. Second Battalion barracks are in the background. Notice that each barracks had its own smaller parade field. Base housing is in the distant background.

**SECOND BATTALION.** Similar construction ensued in the Second Recruit Training Battalion on Panama Street. The pictured recruit barracks are in the vicinity of the present recruit receiving facility on Panama Street.

**RIFLE RANGE BARRACKS.** A small number of the H-style barracks were built at the rifle range. It is the rear or backs of the rifle range barracks that are pictured. Metal fire escapes were later added to the World War II barracks. The barracks were originally painted gray and all barracks by 1955 were shingled in white. Notice the overhead steam pipes and the clothing wash rack.

**PARRIS ISLAND BAND.** First Battalion barracks in this band photograph show a light gray and dark gray trim that was used for barracks on into the early 1950s. Shingles were later added.

**STAFF NONCOMMISSIONED OFFICERS QUARTERS.** Some of the World War II–type buildings served other than recruits. A Staff NCO Quarters for senior enlisted men existed at the end of Panama Street.

**COMMUNICATIONS BUILDING.** Parris Island's growth during World War II required the addition of many services and buildings. The once significant radio communications building within the present base maintenance area and Third Battalion no longer has standing radio towers. Since World War II, the building has been used for many purposes, including those of a recruit training battalion headquarters.

**WALLER BUILDING.** Other now-demolished buildings on Malecon Drive that served numerous purposes was the so-called "Waller Building" and a once-adjacent fire house. Both structures were near the Malecon Drive waterfront and the entrance to Wake Boulevard. The Waller Building had a distinctive large, high slanting roof. Some say it was a secret site during World War II. Others recall that the building was an indoor pistol range but was never used as such. Still others say that a Link flight simulator was housed in the building for training pilots. In the 1950s, the building was used as a recruit training battalion headquarters.

**WORLD WAR II FIRE STATION.** Adjacent to the Waller Building (visible at the left) was a Malecon Drive fire station that was used in the 1950s as a recruit training battalion headquarters. The building also once housed the base provost marshal's office and military police. To the side of the building can be seen a fire hose drying loft. One can see where the engine vehicle doors were later enclosed by the building front entrance way. This 1982 photograph shows the shingles that were placed on older wooden structures on the base since the mid-1950s.

**DEPOT POST OFFICE.** World War II brought tons of mail to Parris Island's recruits. Initially, a post office operated from the present Headquarters and Service building until the current facility was opened on the Boulevard de France. Mail is forwarded to the recruit training battalions. Drill instructors pick up the mail and pass it on to their recruits daily.

**WATER TRANSPORTATION BUILDING.** Additional World War II construction included a water transportation building, officers quarters, and a multiple addition of other buildings. The water transportation building was used during World War II to control river navigation and to assist with the location and recovery of downed aircraft. The building is located on the base dock and has served numerous purposes since World War II.

**WORLD WAR II OFFICERS QUARTERS.** Two sets of commissioned officers quarters are presently located near the base marina. The current quarters, named Osprey Inn, has long served as a bachelor officers quarters (BOQ). The building originally had 40 rooms and faces the base marina on China-Hutung Street.

**OFFICERS QUARTERS.** A smaller, two-story 1942 brick building faces the Beaufort River from Nicaragua Street. In recent years, the building was renovated to quarter VIPs and other base guests.

**OFFICERS CLUB.** Near the two commissioned officers quarters is a rambling white club building that long and exclusively served as the Parris Island Officers Club. The building is located on the site of the old Parris Island quarantine station and faces the Beaufort River. One section of the club building was once adjacent to the base Lyceum. During the 1990s, the club facility was opened to the general base population and was named "Marsh Landing." A more recent designation is "Traditions." A swimming pool and tennis courts are nearby.

**THE TAVERN.** A tavern for enlisted men stood on the corner that is now Memorial Park. The building had two entrances. One part of the club was for corporals and sergeants, and the other side was for privates and privates first class. Large murals adorned the walls of the club. A new club for staff noncommissioned officers was constructed during the war.

**THE SPORTS CENTER.** This two-story World War II building served as an athletic center for Marines. During the late 1950s, recruit strength tests were conducted in the facility. In later years, the still-standing building facade was altered. The building has been used for many purposes. Notice the old street light and bus stop.

**CATHOLIC CHAPEL.** Religious needs were always available on the recruit depot. Some services were conducted in mess halls during the war and in later years. During the 1950s, former mess halls were completely reverted to religious facilities. Pictured is the new Catholic Chapel on Panama Street that was constructed during World War II.

**MEDICAL SERVICES.** Parris Island's medical facilities evolved in size and sophistication as did the overall base. The first base hospital was small compared to the buildings that existed when the Parris Island Hospital was decommissioned on August 31, 1949. Notice the large screened porches where patients could rest before air-conditioning was available.

**PARRIS ISLAND HOSPITAL.** This photograph appears to have been taken after the streets were improved. A bell is seen in front of the United States Naval Hospital building. The bell was later relocated to the modern naval hospital in Beaufort. Notice the nurse in her immaculate white uniform. A recruit wearing a pith helmet and carrying his laundry bag is pictured in the lower left of the photograph.

**HOSPITAL AERIAL VIEW.** The former Parris Island Hospital is seen in the right-center waterfront of this picture. This January 8, 1945 photograph pictures the Boulevard de France across the lower part of the photograph. Notice the *Iron Mike* statue at the curve, the water tank (and shadow), and the enlisted men's tavern on the present site of Memorial Park. The Four Winds Enlisted Club now stands on the far end of the old hospital grounds.

**MODERN HOSPITAL.** The Parris Island Hospital was closed in 1949 and was replaced by the modern and off-base United States Naval Hospital in Beaufort. The hospital was completed on February 1, 1949. The facility receives recruit, dependent, and other military patients.

**REGIMENTAL DISPENSARY.** A number of medical dispensaries were on the World War II base. Some dispensaries were converted to other purposes as they later became obsolete. This regimental dispensary alongside Panama Street later served many purposes. During World War II and the Korean War, recruits received medical shots and other examinations here. The building also served as the Psychiatric Observation Unit (POU). The building no longer stands.

**DISPENSARIES.** One other large brick building that served medical purposes still stands next to the Catholic Chapel on Panama Street. A dispensary was also at the rifle range. The pictured former West End Dispensary was a major facility for recruits and was nearer the parade ground. Notice the former base gas station in the upper left of the photograph. A recruit barbershop and Triangle Post Exchange was near the gas station. These facilities were used on base for many later years.

**PARRIS ISLAND DENTAL DISPENSARY.** The building was the largest dental facility under one single roof during World War II. The huge building served recruits and Marines during three wars. A dental prosthetic laboratory was near the large dispensary. Since 1956, the laboratory has served as the headquarters for the recruit training command. A Federal Credit Union building now occupies the former dental dispensary site and a modern dental facility exists today. Patients entered the Boulevard de France dispensary through the arcade seen near the automobiles on the picture left side. The backside of Second Battalion recruit barracks is seen on the far right side of the picture.

**HYGIENIC BUILDING.** The Hygienic Building was near the large Regimental Dispensary along side Panama Street. Here, recruits received their initial haircut, shower, and other inspections. The facility was later replaced by a modern building on Panama Street.

CLOTHING ISSUE. A corner of the Hygienic Building is seen in this photograph. A metal building constructed after the war served as a recruit clothing issue building for years. Here recruits were fitted for their dress uniforms. The uniforms were picked up by recruit platoons just before boot camp graduation.

BASE LAUNDRY. A base laundry is pictured to the right of a swimming pool bathhouse and a motor transport building is seen to the left. The World War II structures still serve the base.

**FUEL DEPOT.** The former base fuel depot building is another of the many metal World War II facilities that have been razed from the base.

**WORLD WAR II BASE EXCHANGE.** The World War II Base Exchange housed many offices, including a restaurant, snack bar, base library, barber shop, bank, and public affairs office. A lower wing of the building has housed the Douglas Visitors Center for many years.

**SEN. PAUL H. DOUGLAS.** Douglas came to Parris Island as a former college professor after receiving a special age waiver to enlist in the Marine Corps. He was granted an unheard-of full combat classification at the age of 50, and was later decorated in combat. Douglas attained the rank of a lieutenant colonel. He became a United States senator from Illinois after World War II.

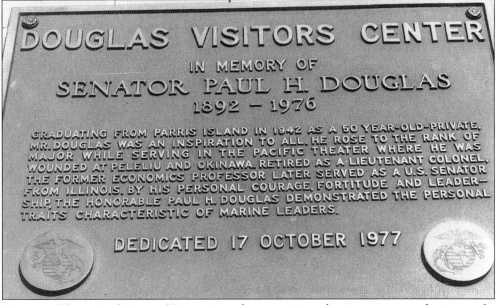

**DOUGLAS VISITORS CENTER**
IN MEMORY OF
**SENATOR PAUL H. DOUGLAS**
1892 – 1976

GRADUATING FROM PARRIS ISLAND IN 1942 AS A 50 YEAR-OLD-PRIVATE, MR. DOUGLAS WAS AN INSPIRATION TO ALL. HE ROSE TO THE RANK OF MAJOR WHILE SERVING IN THE PACIFIC THEATER WHERE HE WAS WOUNDED AT PELELIU AND OKINAWA. RETIRED AS A LIEUTENANT COLONEL, THE FORMER ECONOMICS PROFESSOR LATER SERVED AS A U.S. SENATOR FROM ILLINOIS. BY HIS PERSONAL COURAGE, FORTITUDE AND LEADERSHIP, THE HONORABLE PAUL H. DOUGLAS DEMONSTRATED THE PERSONAL TRAITS CHARACTERISTIC OF MARINE LEADERS.

DEDICATED 17 OCTOBER 1977

**DOUGLAS VISITORS CENTER.** Visitors attending recruit graduations come to the center for information and guidance around the base. Various historical displays have appeared at the center. For some time the Marine Corps memorabilia of Paul Douglas was on display.

**OUTDOOR THEATER VICINITY.** A World War II open-air theater faced Wake Boulevard (foreground) near the junction with Malecon Drive. The former Communications Building is pictured to the right. Part of a now-removed mess hall is visible on the left. Officer's homes were once on the street and numerous recruit battalions used the mess hall and lived in the area that was filled with crude personnel barracks and Quonset huts.

**THE PRESIDENT'S COLOR GUARD.** President Franklin D. Roosevelt visited Parris Island in 1943. This photograph pictures President Roosevelt's color guard and the mass of troops in formation honoring the President. The photograph was taken in front of an open-air theater screen that faced Wake Boulevard. Notice the Waller Building with the high slanted roof that faced Malecon Drive that leads to the main gate. (Courtesy of Michael Lasky.)

**PRESIDENT FRANKLIN D. ROOSEVELT.** President Roosevelt is the most historically significant person to visit Parris Island. The crippled President detrained in Port Royal at a railroad siding about one mile from the main gate. A ramp was built so that his wheel chair could carry him to his convertible automobile that was especially designed for him. Notice the handrails on the windshield frame of the car and elsewhere that the President could use for support. Malecon Drive and Port Royal are in the far distance.

**PARRIS ISLAND TOUR.** President Roosevelt toured much of Parris Island. Thousands lined the depot streets to see their hero who led the nation out of the Great Depression and to victory during World War II. Secret service agents surround the President's car.

**THE POST FARM.** Parris Island supported a massive farm to help feed those who lived on the base. Much of the farm paralleled Wake Boulevard that leads to the Weapons Training Battalion or to the rifle range. As President Roosevelt's entourage drove to the rifle range, the Parris Island swine were slopped to be militarily aligned for the President to see. The President and the Parris Island commanding general chuckled and commented that in the Marine Corps, even swine stand in formation for the President of the United States.

**POST FARM BUILDING.** The base Post Farm was operational from March 1918 until 1950. Parris Island milk bottles are collectors' treasures today. One of the last remaining buildings of the magnificent Post Farm is pictured. The building no longer exists.

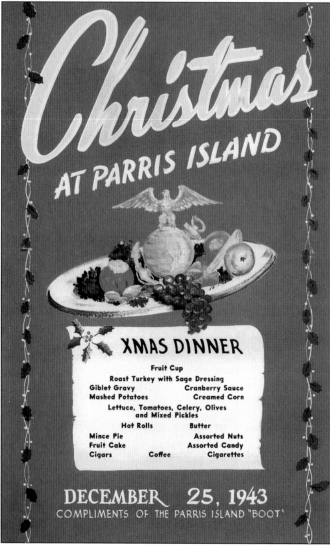

**CHRISTMAS, 1943.** Marines who were once farmers worked the Post Farm. Outstanding dinners were enjoyed by the Marines and United States Navy personnel on holidays or for special events. The base newspaper was named the *Boot* and remains in circulation today.

**THE MOST DANGEROUS WEAPON IN THE WORLD.** This is a photo of a Marine in the making with his rifle and bayonet. He was recruit-trained with the M1Garand rifle that replaced the Springfield '03. The M1 was a semi-automatic weapon and was superior to the infantry rifles used by the enemy. The pith helmet was worn for protection from the South Carolina sun. The corporal appears focused, as does the recruit.

**PVT. STERLING HAYDEN.** The celebrity Hollywood actor of the 1940s and 1950s was a Parris Island recruit in 1943. Notice the recruits are wearing ties during warmer weather. This picture clearly shows the barracks with wooden fire escapes.

**"Hurry Up And Wait!"** Much of life in the military was spent waiting. These World War II recruits appear to be searching for some direction, except for the young man standing at attention in the right of the picture.

IT'S NOT THE
SAND!
NOR THE RAIN!
NOR THE SUN!
IT'S DRILLING IN ALL
THREE!
JUST A 'LUGGIN' MY
"GUN"—
ERR! I MEAN MY
"RIFLE"— SIR!

**Never A "Gun!"** This cartoon figure emphasizes that no matter how severe the hardships, a recruit or Marine never calls his rifle a "gun." To do so could bring down the wrath of a drill instructor (DI) upon an individual or an entire platoon. (Drawing by M. M. Feleming.)

**RECRUIT HOUSING.** World War II recruits lived in metal Quonset huts (left), wooden two-story barracks (center top), or personnel barracks (PBs). One such building is seen at the top far right. The sand parade field and a mess hall are visible at the end of the Quonset hut company street.

**PERSONNEL BARRACKS (PBS).** World War II drill instructor Donald Temple stands near one of the crudely built personnel barracks that once stood in the rifle range and present commissary and Third Recruit Training Battalion areas. Most of the buildings were removed by 1951.

**SWIMMING INSTRUCTION.** The recruit indoor training pool was located at the rifle range. The large metal building was used for years until a modern Olympic-sized facility was constructed near the main station parade ground.

**WOMEN MARINES.** Parris Island is the only base that trains female Marine Corps recruits. Although women Marines date back to World War I, it was not until World War II that they trained collectively on a Marine Corps base. This later photograph shows the women's battalion in its entirety as it was known until a new battalion was constructed for female recruits. Only one of the major buildings pictured remained in 2002. The Ballast Creek Bridge (DI Bridge) is seen spanning Ballast Creek in the top center-right. The Beaufort River is seen in the far upper left.

**OLD AND NEW FEMALE BARRACKS AREAS.** A new facility for women Marines was operational in 1978. The new battalion was built near the old battalion in the large opening identified by the softball field in the photo center. The roadway at the right leads to the old dry dock and commanding general's residence. The road leading to Page Field is seen at the bottom of the photograph.

**MODERN BARRACKS FOR WOMEN MARINES.** This is an early photograph of the contemporary area for female Marines and recruits. Officer housing is seen in the upper part of the photograph, as is the Beaufort River.

**PAGE FIELD.** The Parris Island airfield was operational in 1934 and officially designated a Marine Corps facility in 1935. The field experienced remarkable growth during World War II. The marker honors Capt. Arthur Hallet Page Jr. The Marine aviator was commissioned in 1918 and received numerous flying awards. The St. Paul Minnesota native was killed in a 1930 plane crash. To have greater access to the field from the main station, a bridge was constructed over Ballast Creek (The DI Bridge). Today the Page Field area is mostly used for recruit training exercises.

**PAGE FIELD RUNWAYS.** Port Royal Harbor, the Beaufort River, and the Page Field runways are all prominent in this photograph.

**PAGE FIELD HEADQUARTERS.** It is difficult today to realize that this large headquarters building was at Page Field. Other facilities served the Marines there and many women Marines were assigned to aviation fields.

**MEMORIAL PARK.** An enlisted men's club once occupied this site and was known as The Tavern. When the club building was razed, the area was designated Memorial Park. Several monuments are here to honor the World War II Defense Battalions that trained on Parris Island. Along with several other plaques and markers is the statue *Molly Marine*. The original 1943 statue is in New Orleans and a replica was created for Parris Island. The base is the only Marine Corps station that trains female Marine recruits. *Molly Marine* is the work of Mexican sculptor Enrique Alferez. The statue was dedicated on October 23, 1999.

**DRILL INSTRUCTOR MONUMENT.** A contemporary monument to honor both male and female drill instructors stands adjacent to the Parade Deck. Former 1957 recruits, Jim Whalen and Ted Hetland, admire the imposing piece.

**LT. ROGER BLOOD.** At the end of World War II and into the 1950s, a number of monuments were placed on the base to honor the sacrifices of the Marines lost in war. Near the statue of *Iron Mike* is a fountain dedicated to the memory of First Lt. Roger Blood and "to all Marines trained at Parris Island who are among the honored dead of World War II." Blood enlisted in 1942, was commissioned in 1943, and was killed in action in 1944.

**IWO JIMA FLAG RAISING.** The most obvious base monument stands on the parade field and was dedicated in 1952. A larger Arlington National Cemetery statue was sculpted by Felix de Weldon. This picture was taken from a famous 1945 Pulitzer prize-winning photograph by Joe Rosenthal. Lesser known photographs were also made. The monument shows five Marines and one United States Navy hospital corpsman raising the American flag atop Mt. Suribachi on Iwo Jima, on February 23, 1945. The photograph shows the original size of the parade field and a World War II barracks in the background. The statue obscures a large open-air theater screen.

**IWO JIMA MONUMENT.** The Pacific Island battle took the lives of over 6,000 Americans in less than one month. Three of the six flag-raisers were killed on Iwo Jima. Two of the men were Parris Island Marines. In respect to the men on Iwo Jima, Adm. Chester W. Nimitz stated, "Uncommon Valor Was A Common Virtue."

IN HONOR AND IN MEMORY OF
THE MEN OF THE
UNITED STATES MARINE CORPS
WHO HAVE GIVEN
THEIR LIVES TO THEIR COUNTRY
SINCE 10 NOVEMBER 1775

**MONUMENT DEDICATION.** Although the magnificent statue is commonly believed to be an Iwo Jima or World War II Memorial, it is actually dedicated to all Marines. November 10, 1775 is celebrated as the birthday of the Marine Corps.

**SGT. MAJOR JIGGS (1921–1927).** The Marine Corps favors the Bulldog as a mascot. Sergeant Jiggs was one of the most famous "Devil Dogs." The dog traveled more than 100,000 miles and most likely visited Parris Island. Secretary of the Navy Curtis D. Wilbur promoted Jiggs to the rank of sergeant major in 1924. (Courtesy of Mrs. Rachael Taipalus.)

**MIKE.** Mike's impressive gravestone is the oldest standing monument on the Parris Island base. It is located adjacent to the former dry dock and near the commanding general's home. The mascot saw combat in Vera Cruz, Mexico in 1914, and came with the first Marines from Virginia to Parris Island in 1915. He was known by half of the Marine Corps by the time of his death in 1916. The inscription reads "Our Mascot, 1905–MIKE–1916, Service, Honest And Faithful."

**MASCOT CEMETERY.** Some of the canines buried near Mike had their gravestones moved to a Horse Island bluff that overlooks Archer's Creek.

**Cpl. Iron Mike.** Depot bulldogs are cared for by individual Marines and others. Many of the base mascots lived in the Parris Island brig. All mascots are popular at ceremonies and recruit graduation parades. Cpl. Iron Mike is posed at the Iwo Jima Monument. (Picture by Cpl. D.L. King, USMC.)

**THOR.** When Maj. Gen. Stephen G. Olmstead pointed his finger at Thor, the 1985 bulldog went for it! The mascot received a nonpunitive letter of caution, and got off the hook by being ordered to assist several local organizations in charitable campaigns. The son of Thor is pictured with his dad.

**DEPOT FLOODING.** It is not rare to have flooding on the island, especially following severe storms and hurricanes. Notice the water is knee-high to the Recruiters School Marines. The mascot seems to enjoy the swim. (Courtesy of Capt. Sam Head, USMC, Retired.)

**RECRUITERS SCHOOL.** This photograph was taken of the Class One, Parris Island Recruiters School in 1947. (Courtesy of Capt. Sam Head, USMC, Retired.)

PLATOON I

THIRD RECRUIT BATTALION
S. SGT. D. E. SULLIVAN
MARCH 23rd 1949

M. C. R. D., PARRIS ISLAND, S.C.
SGT. B. J. SCHULTZ
PHOTO BY. Mass.

**RETURN OF THE WOMEN MARINES.** Women were integrated on a permanent basis into the Marine Corps in 1948. Platoon 1 was photographed on March 23, 1949. At this time distaff recruits were in the Third Recruit Training Battalion. The battalion is presently designated the Fourth Battalion.

# *Three*

# PARRIS ISLAND
## 1950–PRESENT

*The Recruit Depot once again experienced tremendous growth during the Korean and Vietnam Wars. Yet, by the mid-1950s, many of the older base buildings were coming down as new brick barracks were planned for recruits. All Quonset huts and World War II wooden barracks were eventually removed to give Parris Island its present appearance. The recruit training program also changed to permit more individual physical training and platoon field exercises.*

CHANGING PARRIS ISLAND. The c. 1980 picture shows the modern recruit brick barracks and many of the older World War II recruit barracks that faced Panama Street. The former full-sized parade deck is prominent. The former recruit Triangle Post Exchange is visible in the lower left-center of the picture. Many of these buildings were soon razed or replaced. (Photograph by Ernest Ferguson.)

**YEMASSEE, SOUTH CAROLINA**. Yemassee remained the arrival place for recruits until 1965. Recruits are now flown to Charleston and then bussed to Parris Island.

**RAW RECRUITS.** Drill instructors once received their platoons "fresh off the bus." These brand new recruits are herded along and being stripped of any civilian individuality that may remain. The silver helmet liners were to reduce any chance of heat-related accidents. Notice the full size of the parade ground at this time. Drill instructors were issued campaign hats in 1956.

**FOOTPRINTS.** In the early 1960s, footprints were painted on the pavement in front of the recruit receiving barracks. The images were to assist the new recruit in learning where to stand in formation. New sets of footprints are in front of the modern receiving barracks. The modern indoor instruction swimming pool is in the background.

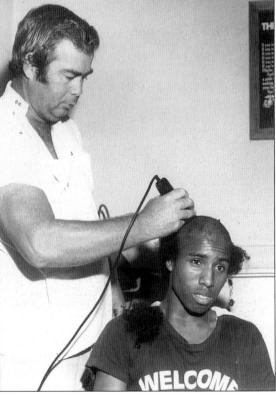

**PARRIS ISLAND HAIRCUT.** The new recruit in the "welcome" shirt seems to be asking, "What have I done?"

**WORLD WAR II BARRACKS.** Through the Korean War (1950–1953) and into the Vietnam War era, many recruits lived in the older World War II barracks. Notice the barracks exterior is shingled and there are metal fire escapes.

**TENTS.** Korean War recruits often lived in Quonset huts and in tents. During the war, tents were placed on most any available space. This photograph pictures recruit tents along the Boulevard de France, near the present Douglas Visitors Center. The largest number of recruits to train on Parris Island at any one time was 21,540 men in 1952 during the Korean War. The number surpassed the World War II number of recruits in training at any one time.

**QUONSET HUTS.** Pictured here are two drill instructors standing near Quonset huts. The metal huts covered the rifle range area and the present Third Battalion area on the base. Notice that the two herringbone utility uniforms differ. The 1953–1954 DI pictured on the right still wears the World War II utility uniform with metal buttons and large pockets.

**DRILL INSTRUCTORS.** Until late 1956, most lower ranking and single drill instructors lived in reserved quarters of barracks, huts, and tents near their recruits. Such quarters also served as the DI duty office. Pictured is a drill instructor's iron frame bed. Notice the towel and laundry bag on the rear of the bunk, along with the DI's duty holster and belt. Locker boxes and wall lockers were available for instructors, too.

**DRILL INSTRUCTOR DUTY ROOM.**
This DI duty room has a double bunk
for instructors. A field desk is seen in
the lower right of the picture. Training
schedules and such are posted on
the clipboards and a weekly calendar
is on the wall.

**CAMPAIGN HATS.** A
formal Marine Corps
Drill Instructor School
was opened at the San
Diego and Parris Island
Recruit Depots in 1952.
Drill instructors were
issued campaign hats in
1956. Before then, the
utility hat was worn. In
this picture, two drill
instructors are wearing
newly issued campaign
hats. The third wears
the baseball style utility
hat. Notice the DI duty
holster and belt that was
used by drill instructors in
the 1950s.

**RECRUIT BARRACKS.** This barracks interior was standard for the World War II H design. It was unlikely that a bugler played reveille in a squad bay. Notice the M1 rifles are in racks. Packs, towels, and laundry bags are affixed to the bunks. A locker box for each recruit is seen, and shoes were neatly aligned on each side of the bunk.

**Recruit Barracks.** A more current open view of a World War II barracks squad bay is pictured here. Notice the stanchions that were only in lower squad bays. The bar in the center of the picture could be used to hang uniforms. Rifles are affixed to the frame bunk, and fluorescent lights are installed.

**MODERN RECRUIT BARRACKS.** All World War II recruit barracks were eventually razed and replaced with brick structures, beginning in the male Third Battalion as early as 1958. This massive recruit barracks dwarfs the older wooden buildings that harbored Marines of World War II, the Korean War, and the Vietnam War.

**PAGE FIELD DI BARRACKS.** Following a tragic 1956 training mishap and misconduct of a drill instructor that resulted in the drowning of six recruits, DIs were moved from living in recruit barracks near their platoons. Drill instructor quarters were moved to Page Field buildings AS-33 and AS-14. The two barracks housed officers during World War II. The roadway in the upper right of the photograph leads to the main station and spans Ballast Creek. The two buildings no longer exist.

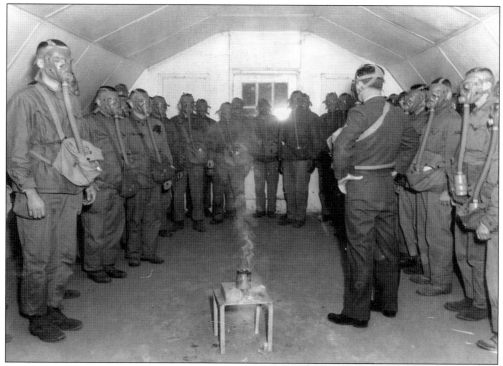

**GAS CHAMBER.** Recruit training includes an introduction to gas masks and the effects of harmless gas. The drill was mostly conducted inside a metal Quonset hut, where recruits marched around a canister of fuming tear gas. At some point, an instructor could order the masks to be removed and for the recruits to sing *The Marines' Hymn*. All nostrils and sinuses were clear at the end of the drill. The effects of even a harmless gas were learned and the event was never forgotten.

**FIRE WATCH!** Recruits were assigned fire watch duties during their training. The exercise taught them how to stand security watches and to be alert for any irregular activities, especially fire. The fire watch duty was assigned at the discretion of the drill instructor and the recruit immediately reported when summoned.

**CLOTHESLINE WATCH.** Recruits were also assigned clothesline watch. The sentry guarded a platoon's clothes from theft. Clothes were washed on a concrete table with a scrub brush and hung from lines with small pieces of rope called "tie-ties." The bleachers were for instructional purposes. This lone recruit is wearing his poncho to protect him from the rain.

**CHRISTMAS AT PARRIS ISLAND.** A 1956 First Battalion mess hall is decorated for the Christmas season.

**BEAUFORT RIVER.** The Beaufort River (left) and Port Royal Sound (top right) are shown in this *c.* 1958 photograph. The former Parris Island Hospital buildings remain standing. A Page Field runway is visible in the upper right of the picture. The picture shows the juxtaposition of the Lyceum, former commanding officers headquarters, Buildings 10 and 11, the dry dock, and part of the Headquarters and Service Battalion. The building at right-center with the dark, rounded roof was the base bakery.

**BOULEVARD DE FRANCE.** The Iwo Jima Monument appears white in this mid-1950s photograph that shows part of the parade field. The large field in the center of the photograph is now the First Recruit Training Battalion Physical Training Field. The single white building was a toilet and bath building for Korean War recruits, who were quartered in hundreds of tents in this base area. Second Battalion barracks appear in the lower right corner of the photograph.

**THE LYCEUM.** The former dry dock machine shop has served many purposes. For years, it was a base theater and a place for boxing matches and indoor assemblies. Tickets were taken at the front door when admission was no longer free. Another theater was at the rifle range. Notice the antique street lamp.

**THE DI.** Jack Webb starred in and produced the hit movie, *The DI*. Webb's company, Mark VII Limited, produced numerous television and big-screen movies. Webb is best known as Sgt. Joe Friday, LAPD, Badge 714 in his successful radio show, television show, and motion picture *Dragnet*. Webb was tailored for the stern drill instructor role he played in *The DI* and the 1957 movie is one of his best performances. (Courtesy of Daniel Moyer.)

**THE DI.** The story was about a Parris Island drill instructor and his concern for an errant recruit. Although the story locale was Parris Island, the film was actually made in southern California. The picture offers an excellent example of recruit barracks and dress in 1957. (Courtesy of Daniel Moyer.)

113

**THREE RECRUIT TRAINING BATTALIONS.** This remarkable picture, c. 1957, shows Third Battalion Quonset huts along the top. Several wooden Second Battalion barracks are seen center left. Only one First Battalion barracks is pictured to the bottom right. The battalion for women recruits is not pictured. The imprinted open field in the picture lower left once housed tents and Quonset huts. Notice the recruit Triangle Post Exchange (PX) and the depot gas station in the center of the picture. A World War II open-air theater was in the open field. It is here that President Roosevelt addressed Parris Island's Marines in 1943. The road on the upper left of the picture leads to the rifle range. The road on the right side of the photograph leads to Horse Island and the base main gate.

**THE WAR MEMORIAL BUILDING AND PARRIS ISLAND MUSEUM.** This impressive building was completed in 1952. It was designed to serve as a recreational facility, but was later converted to house the Parris Island Museum. The outside brick walls are adorned with the names of Marine Corps battles and campaigns.

**DEPOT RESTAURANT.** One of several base commercial restaurants faces Panama Street and the Parris Island Museum. This building has been renovated many times. (Photograph by Ernest Ferguson.)

**GEN. RANDOLPH C. BERKELEY BRIDGE.** The modern Archer's Creek Bridge was dedicated on September 30, 1954. The smaller wooden and steel bridges were removed and the causeway was slightly altered. This photograph reveals the route of the former bridges made visible by the telephone poles and the missing section of the road. General Berkeley commanded the Parris Island base from 1933 to 1936.

**WOMEN MARINE BARRACKS AND DEPOT MARINA.** The barracks for female recruits and women Marines are seen in the center of this mid-1950s photograph. A ramp at the base marina clearly shows the site where seaplanes once exited the water. The metal building to the left center was a former hangar.

**INSPECTION.** These ladies seem to be far advanced in their recruit training. Notice the old iron bunk frames in the photograph.

**WOMEN MARINES CLUB.** This small building faced the base marina and served as a club for women Marines.

**STAFF NONCOMMISSIONED OFFICERS CLUB.** This former club is pictured in the lower left of the photograph and was constructed during World War II. The photograph shows the Second and First Battalion barracks and the huge parade field. On the field and at the distant end of the center street is the screen of the post–World War II, open-air theater that was once so prominent on the base.

**MODERN BASE THEATER.** The historic Lyceum was replaced as the main indoor theater by the end of the 1950s. The present base theater is pictured in the lower left part of the picture. The Parris Island Headquarters Building, seen in the center of the photograph, was constructed during World War II. At this time Memorial Park was still the site of The Tavern, an enlisted men's club. The Beaufort River and the former dry dock are visible in the top of the photograph.

**PHYSICAL TRAINING (PT).** During the late 1950s, a greater emphasis was placed on individual physical training. Here, recruits are lifting metal logs while doing sit-ups. The exercise builds strength and teamwork. Notice the drill instructor to the left. The recruits are in their PT uniforms as two physical training instructors supervise the exercise. The onlooking officers are in the Korean Marine Corps.

**THE RIFLE RANGE.** Marksmanship remains a primary part of being a Marine and every Marine is a rifleman. Recruits in the foreground are seen "snapping in" or "dry-firing" to learn shooting positions and the habits of outstanding shooters. An instruction shed is at the left and the firing range is in the distance.

**THE M16 RIFLE.** Female recruits must qualify with the military rifle in the modern Marine Corps.

BAYONET TRAINING AT PARRIS ISLAND

**BAYONET TRAINING.** A close combat instructor teaches the bayonet to a recruit platoon. Second battalion wooden recruit barracks and metal sheds remain at the time of this 1980s photograph. (Picture by Ernest Ferguson.)

**WASH RACK.** The day of the concrete wash rack, scrub brush, metal pail, and clotheslines watches for recruits are no more. Barracks 761 stands proudly in the background of this photograph. It was the last of the World War II barracks to be razed at the rifle range.

**FIRST RECRUIT TRAINING BATTALION PLATOON AND BARRACKS, 1997.** Parris Island's modern barracks have washers and dryers and recruits have some laundry service. The monstrous, modern barracks dwarf former Parris Island recruit barracks.

**MODERN RECRUIT TRAINING.** The care of one's self and equipment, building confidence, and learning how to fight have always been the challenges given to Marine Corps recruits. Pugil stick training builds confidence and develops bayonet and close combat skills. Recruits are heavily protected and the short bouts are closely supervised. An instructor is seen in the photograph.

**"THE SLIDE FOR LIFE."** Modern recruit training demands more personal physical training then ever before. The pictured platform is reached by climbing the net suspended to the two poles. A recruit in this 1982 photograph is seen descending a rope over a body of water that cushions any fall. The obstacle builds stamina and confidence.

122

**CLEANING RIFLES.** Marine recruits are taught their rifle is their best friend. Keeping one's rifle in excellent condition has always been emphasized to recruits. Recruits in this photograph are cleaning the M16 rifle. Notice the short haircuts, locker boxes, camouflage field uniforms, and the newer type barracks metal frame bunks.

**DRILL.** Close order drill is considered essential for desired discipline. Two drill instructors (DIs) are seen with this platoon. The sword carried by the instructor to the right of the picture is for ceremonial purposes.

**WOMEN RECRUITS.** A female drill instructor examines women recruits at inspection arms, presenting their M16 rifle. In 1996 women drill instructors were authorized to wear the campaign hat.

**RIFLE INSPECTION.** A senior female staff noncommissioned officer appears to have found dirt on a recruit's rifle. Women Marines in the modern Marine Corps have more opportunities than ever, and have attained the general rank.

**OBSTACLE COURSES.** Women recruits are taught to have the same skills and confidence of the male recruits. A determined recruit is pictured in the photograph with her concerned instructor on one of the Parris Island obstacle courses.

**FOURTH RECRUIT TRAINING BATTALION.** Parris Island is the only female recruit training base in the Marine Corps. The modern female training complex is seen in the picture on the lower right. The white building to the top right of the battalion buildings is the Drill Instructor School. The black upper-center parade deck is visible in the picture.

**PRESIDENT RONALD REAGAN.** President Ronald Regan visited Parris Island in 1986 and found that modern training continued to produce outstanding Marines.

**RETURNING TO PARRIS ISLAND.** Hundreds of former recruits return to Parris Island each year to remember their boot camp experience. It has been stated that the Marine Corps is the largest fraternity in the world and the recruit depots at Parris Island and San Diego have made it so. Former Marine Raider and DI Lou Adams is seen with his depot host at the 9th World War II Drill Instructors Reunion. (Courtesy of Sam Cosman.)

**WORLD WAR II PARRIS ISLAND DRILL INSTRUCTORS.** The men in this photograph (with honorary exceptions) were heroes of the World War II Pacific War. They consist of judges, teachers, successful businessmen, and much more. Although some of them bare the wounds of the war, they always long to return to Parris Island. (Courtesy of Sam Cosman.)

**PLATOON PHOTOGRAPH.** Each and every recruit looks forward to the day that a platoon photograph is taken because it means that graduation is only a few days away. This 1953 platoon and its drill instructors wear starched khaki uniforms. Recruit graduation pictures were taken behind and near the current Douglas Visitors Center for years.

**GRADUATION.** Graduation gives the recruit the right to be addressed as a United States Marine. In this *c.* 1995 picture, one sees the old white First Battalion wooden barracks alongside the modern brick barracks. The once sand parade ground has been reduced in size. Such ceremonies are a far cry from ones of the past, which were designed to be brief to hasten new Marines off to war. However, as in the past, Parris Island will always be up to the task of producing Marines to defend the United States of America. (Photograph by Ernest Ferguson.)